GW00645476

New Milton

in old picture postcards

by
A.T. Lloyd

European Library – Zaltbommel/Netherlands

Fifth edition: 1994

GB   ISBN 90 288 3315 3 / CIP

© 1985 European Library – Zaltbommel/Netherlands

INTRODUCTION

RAILWAY turns MILTON Village into a Town, NEW MILTON.

Barton has been known world-wide since Brander's 1766 book on its fossils, and Sir J. Evans in 1897 made pre-historians aware of the wealth of its palaeolithic remains. Bronze Age urns were found from 1910 and Celtic gold coins since. Milton has a rare moated farm site, and 300 mediaeval deeds survive for those lands held since 1435 by Winchester College. From the time of the first Saxo-Jutish settlements here, about 750 A.D., the area was of scattered farms ('tons'). Details for eight of these manors were given in Domesday, 1086. Milton ('middle farm') by 1270 was the centre of a parish, incorporating Milton, Barton (2), Ashley (2), Fernhill, Bashley and Wootton. The parish bounds, after an area west of Walkford stream was lopped off in 1843, remain as those of New Milton town (5,800 acres).

The village in 1880 had blacksmiths, a bootmaker, saddler, baker/grocer (from 1856), coastguards, a butcher from 1861 and a policeman. The lanes were of cart-width and at large dips there were fords. Fernhill Estate had gates across the main roads. Southern Lane led to the Coastguards', Dilly Lane from the Green to a farm. Barton and Becton Lanes were the only ways to Barton Court.

The arrival of the railway main line in 1888 through the village changed everything, creating a new focal point for shops and houses as 'MILTON' Station was nearly a mile from the old centre. The College sold lands near the station and Barton fields became available for houses when Mr. Dent died. In 1881 the population was 1,489; in 1931: 5,300; now 20,000. Sea and sun were the attractions.

Mr. Wyeth of Winchester saw the possibilities; he built Milton Hotel and Hall, etc., near the station. Barton Court by 1898 had a golf course from the hotel. In 1900 the Water Tower replaced most wells. By 1895 Mrs. Newhook's shop near the station sold stamps. She added the prefix 'New' to her sub Post Office; this was adopted by the railway in 1897. So *NEW* Milton was born.

Half a dozen brick kilns used the railway to send bricks to Bournemouth, etc. After 1880 no new cob cottage was built; a few remain, like Jordan's, butcher; some are masked in brick. Ashley Baptists built a fine chapel in 1899 to replace that of 1817; an 'offspring' was erected in Milton in 1910, three years after Bashley's Anglican chapel was put up. Ashley Anglicans had, in turn, two Mission rooms, then a chapel hut (1904), replaced by a new St. Peter's in 1956. Two of the three pubs were rebuilt by 1905. From 1901 the sub Post Office was on Whitefield corner, standing alone till a few shops reached to the

Unionist Club. Hayward's farm stood till 1927; by that time the east side of Station Road was filled with substantial houses to the cross roads.

The 1836 National School by 'The George' stayed in use till 1919, when it moved to ex-Army huts in Gore Road. Wootton School was destroyed by fire in 1914. In Baptist Ashley the school built in 1879 was non-denominational at the insistence of the Hon. Auberon Herbert.

The village was extremely lucky in having a much-loved Rector, J. Kelsall, 1897-1924. His influence pervaded all aspects of life. The Baptist parson, Mr. Edginton, was also a man respected throughout the village. They sometimes exchanged pulpits. Largely through the Rector's drive the Laundry by the Pound became an Institute and Whitefield was bought as a Recreation Ground to commemorate the war.

Till 1886 the inovator, the Hon. A. Herbert, lived at Ashley Arnewood; from about that time the scholarly Miss Bateson ran her unique plant nursery at Bashley, and from 1913 to 1924 the prolific writer Laurence Housman lived at Ashley.

The Great War brought the world to the village. 250 guests at Barton Court Hotel were replaced by British and, later, Indian troops, housed in huts, trying to convalesce at 'Breezy Barton', the name the British troops gave to their little paper. The obelisk commemorates the Indians.

In the 1920s a thousand homes were built, so the parish in 1926 became an Urban District. It tarred and drained the main roads, bought the sea front and replaced gas lighting with electricity. The Roman Catholic Church was built, 1927, and the parish church was extended to the east in 1928, the year that saw the birth of 'The New Milton Advertiser'. The pleasant situation of the village caused the founding of private Preparatory Schools, occupying land now of great value.

Mr. Kirkman, the first chemist, set up a Fire Brigade by 1910, using his motor cycle side-car to ferry hoses, etc. The Chawners and others founded Operatic and Theatrical Societies. Football, cricket and tennis clubs etc. were formed. The 'Scala' provided 'silent' films for ten years till 'The Waverley' went up in 1929. By that time everyone had bikes and some had cars. Life had more to offer.

Despite opposition, the Urban District Council was incorporated into Lymington Borough from 1932-1974; since then it has been part of the New Forest District, with Town status for New Milton since 1979.

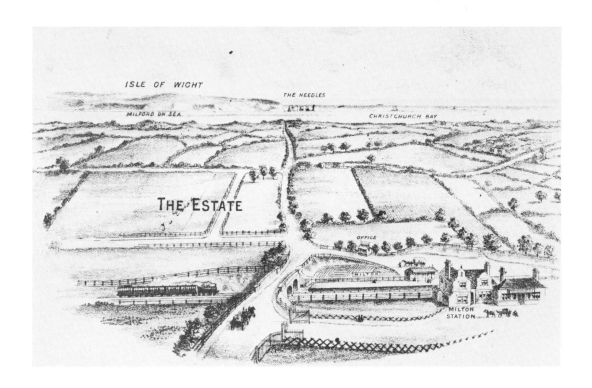

1. This bird's eye sketch appeared on the cover of the Sale Catalogue for Milton Park Estate in 1892. The Station, 'MILTON, for Milford-on-Sea', had been built in 1886. The first public train stopped here on 6 March 1888. On 1 May 1897 the station name was changed to 'NEW MILTON'. The whole area to the coast was for growing cereal crops. The land for sale, in the foreground, had belonged to Winchester College since Fromond's gift of 1420 was ratified. These were the Fernhill Estates, with documents back to 1190s. The Manor house is out of sight, directly below the artist's view point. Just over the railway line the Water Tower was built in 1900 on the left. Whitefield, in the centre right, has Hayward's farm and Legg's cottage; otherwise all is empty to the village centre and church. Part of the 'x' fence remained till 1960.

BRITISH CINERARY URN
(& CONTENTS)
FOUND ON
- BARTON COMMON -
MARCH 1910.
BRONZE PERIOD
RESTORED BY MR J. ACUTT.

2. This Bronze Age bucket urn, exactly like one found by General Pitt-Rivers on his estate, was dug up by Mr. Kitcher, a roadman, in 1910 on Barton Common. Mr. J. Acutt, shown with the congealed mass that was a body, repaired the urn, which in the mid-1930s was the main exhibit in Brigden's Museum in Station Road. When war came the 'mass' and two bronze beads were sent to Lymington, but the urn was smashed. Four urns were found near Dilly Lane in 1927, but none survives. Over 100 palaeolithic flints have been found at Barton and Ashley. A flint knife, two neolithic hammer heads, mesolithic flints and Roman coin have been found, as well es five gold Celtic coins and a mediaeval horse-terret on the beach. The terret bears the arms of de Bohun, Earl of Hereford.

3. The village centre from the air about 1926. Southern Lane leads to the Green, with Joy's sub Post Office on the left of 'The Wheatsheaf'. Then comes the grocer's, Brownen's smithy and house, 'The George' stands in front of the cob butcher's shop, with the Poor House (1796-1836) where lived till recently descendants of J. Cook, a railway ganger of 1880s. On the road island is the National School, 1836-1919, then the Parish Hall till removed in 1931. The long thatched house to the north-east was the home of Mr. Bushby and Mr. Preston. Now the Arts' Centre stands there, using the Civil Defence building erected after the Second World War. The field belongs to the Junior and Infant Schools. From 1960 the Gore Secondary School, now Arnewood Comprehensive, has had the land behind the churchyard, just shown on the left. Near the top is Hobart Road (1906 Liberal victor); '1909' date is on the shops. Facing south is No. 100 of cob, later faced in brick; it dates from 1834.

4. This photo shows the interior of the church of St. Mary Magdalene about 1905, showing the brick nave and chancel of the 1832 rebuilding. Since the second rebuilding of 1928 only the right hand wall and window have survived of the view shown. The tower of about 1695 stands, with its theatrical memorial to Thomas White, whose original 'Andrea Ferrara' sword is encased nearby. He died in 1720. Till the Dissolution, Milton church – first noted in 1270 – was linked with Christchurch Priory; since then the vicar of Milford has appointed the cleric, who became called Rector in 1867. The small photo is of the Reverend J. Kelsall (Rector 1897-1924). He was an expert in ornithology and in inspiring enthusiasm in everyone he met.

MILTON CHURCH

5. Photo of the church from the north. This area since 1932 has been the site of the Church Hall and parking space. In the hall garden the caretaker, Mr. T. Selby, dug up a 'doughnut'-shaped Neolithic hammer head. He it was who in 1931 revived the Scout troop, begun in 1909 by Mr. Hambro and Mr. Paris. The church was extended eastwards in 1928, emphasising round arches and a barrel vault. Sebastian Comper, son of Sir Ninian, incorporated the pointed 1832 style with the rounded in his northern Lady Chapel extension in 1958. The original entrance was on the south-west end of the nave. The Registers begin in 1654. 'Miltoniana' by Kelsall and A. Paris lists the church wardens and Poor Law overseers from 1712 to 1841. They quote from the books of the Overseers of the Poor and Highways, and some Settlement Orders. I have eight names of curates (from 1509) before the list given in the church. The title of Rector was taken in 1867.

6. This photo shows 'The George' inn before it was knocked down in 1904. It has indeed a Georgian look. Outside are the hosts, Mr. and Mrs. Charles Taylor. (He died in 1906, having seen the new 'George' rise.) Further back is shown the butcher's shop of Mr. Topp; this is of cob. Mr. George Topp came here in 1860 and at first used to drive cattle from miles away to be slaughtered here. Once the 1888 line was open he used to have half a dozen cattle and a few sheep brought by train; it is not known if he ever used the 1847 line with its station at Holmsley less than a mile north of the parish. Mr. Topp was 95 when he died. Since then, his cob shop has been run by Mr. C. Rushford and now by Mr. Jordan.

7. This is the village centre, looking east, as it was about 1904. The old 'George' is shown behind the horse. The Green is unenclosed. Out of sight is the school. At the centre stands the home and shop of George Witt, who died in 1917, leaving son Cecil as bootmaker and son Sid as saddler. On the right is the thatched stable and bakery-grocery shop built in 1854 by Charles Peckham. The Witts extended the top part of their shop later; their buildings were removed in 1966 to make way for the 1967 round-about. To the left is the smithy of Mr. Brownen and his home; the smithy was pulled down in April 1954, the house many years before. A member of the family now has a metal shop in Old Milton Road. As boys the Witt brothers used to visit their aunt, laundry-woman at the farm then at the end of Dilly Lane, then drive in a stake at the cliff top so they could bathe from Dent's private beach. The farm was pulled down in the 1890s.

OLD VILLAGE MILTON.

8. This photo by W. East was taken for the 1910 Guide. It shows 'The George' of 1905, which date is finely displayed in the brickwork. The smith's cottage is to the left. At the centre stands the school of 1836, with the roadway — where the children played — on either side. The school was pulled down in the spring of 1931 and re-opened in Gore road huts. Notice that the Green now has strong boundary posts and that the Witt family has added to the northern section of their property. Publicans at 'The George' in the 1880s: W. Bell; 1890s: C. Taylor; 1906: Mrs. Taylor, then F. Dowding. At 'The Wheatsheaf' in the 1880s: E. Turner; in 1890s: J. Strutt, who was also cab proprietor, followed by A. Oakley. At 'The Rising Sun' in the 1880s: W. Moore; 1890s: J. Foot, then J. Carpenter, followed by A. Tanner. The 1859 Directory lists G. Guy at the 'Victoria' in Bashley.

9. This probably depicts Empire Day parade just before the First World War, as there is an army officer behind the girl receiving the flag. The tree planted to commemorate the 1911 coronation is behind the prominent group. Southern Lane was then usually called Thousand Lane – possibly indicating the number of paces to the Coastguard Cottages. The Cox family lived in the larger house now occupied by Johnson's, chemists; the thatched cottage then belonged to Mrs. Bell. Just visible is the turning left to the mediaeval moated area, excavated by Mrs. Hurst in 1956. On the right is a shed and behind, in the trees, Milton Manor, already in a delapidated state; it had Gothick windows. Moat Lane was the north end of Dilly Lane from the village to Barton Farm. Mrs. Hurst's excavation report is in 'Journal of the Archaeological Association', volume XXX, 1967 (21 pages).

"Can the little chap walk?"

"Oh, yes; he's been walking now for five months."

"What a long way he must have come!"

10. This sketch of the village sub Post Office was done for the national magazine 'Winter's Pie' in 1922. It correctly names the official as F.J. Joy, member of the family that built Bournemouth Arcade and that owned the Naish Estate. The Post Office stood to the west of 'The Wheatsheaf', an area now used for parking. The artist, Mr. Starr Wood, lived in one of the Coastguard Cottages in Barton Lane. Old Milton's sub Post Office is now in the parade opposite the Wheatsheaf Garage, and Barton has two sub Post Offices. The main Post Office in New Milton was built in early 18th century style, with urns on the parapet and with a broken pedimented door case, in 1933, as one of the last line of shops on the west side of Station Road. All the shopping developments in the road since have been on the other side, which used to be residential. Much has been designed and built by the firm, McCarthy and Stone, north of the 1966 lights.

11. Mr. Charles Peckham was the village baker, grocer and mealman. His wife was a Lunn from Brockenhurst. Two young bakers stand at the yard entrance to the thatched stables. Mr. Peckham is shown indistinctly behind. Mr. Peckham's father built this shop in 1854. It is now used by a photo-copying company. Another photo shows one son, George, with his delivery van marked 'Steam bakery, Milton'. He went to Canada. A daughter married Mr. N. Caslake, of the art metal-work family; he was an ice manufacturer, supplier of hotels. Next to 'The Wheatsheaf' was another grocer's shop, run by Chipperfield, later by A. Kemsley, then by Mr. Britnell. Their shop, which had a central door, is now incorporated into the 'Wheatsheaf' front. In 1910 Chipperfield's was a typical village store, selling grocery on one side and drapery on the other.

12. This shows Old Milton Road, just north of the old Poor House and school. On the left is the wall of Mr. Hunt's cottage, then comes the double cottage occupied by the Peckham and Compton families, with Dodge's house next. These have all gone, replaced till 1985 by Ingrem's lorry park. The taller semi-detached house of the Sherred and Drew families still stands, as does 'Kerri' (No. 100) facing south, where Mr. Selby used to live. This is of cob, built by 1834, later masked in brick; Mrs. Lovell has sold it this year, 1985. On the opposite side, south of where now stands a bakery, was a tiny cottage, often taken by newly-weds, as Mrs. Saunders told me. As a school girl she saw the first train come through, but died just before the last steam train of 1967. Her last cottage faced the school; it was pulled down, with the Witt's house, to make the garden-rockery at the roundabout in 1967.

13. The Walkford stream is shown in flood at Chewton before the bridge was built in 1901. The Cement and Concrete Association acknowledge the bridge here as the earliest reinforced concrete bridge in England. Mr. H. Cheyney lived in the house on the right; family tradition is that the bricks on the cart were the first load for the bridge. Parish records refer to the footbridges here and over the Danes Stream — west and east parish bounds. Since 1974 Chewton has also been the County boundary. When much of the beach was private, the path down the Bunny beside the Mill (used till 1908) was a favourite Sunday walk. Thatched cottages out of view on the right were demolished in 1958. In 1780 riding officer Bursey was murdered at his door by smugglers here. Records in London give all the details. Chewton means 'Cifa's farm'; Walkford may mean 'cloth walkers' ford'.

14. This fine photo taken very soon after this historic reinforced bridge was built in 1901, shows the cascading water on the south side, with a view of the brick structure and roadway parapet. In 'The Christchurch Times' in 1904 there is a complaint by the owner (General) the Hon. E. Stuart-Wortley about the amount of litter left by people who used this pleasant walk beside the stream to the beach. Fifty yards away, at the top of the hill, there is the Milestone for the turnpiked road. Since 1974 the stream is the Counties' boundary and the bridge is the responsibility of the two authorities. The present extensive Naish Farm Caravan Park began when Mr. J. Burry let out two tin huts for the summer; one was his shepherd's hut, the other a storage hut. Naish should keep its old pronunciation, 'Nash'.

15. Henry Cheyney, his wife Fanny and eight children lived in the house shown on no. 13. He died in 1928, aged 78. His wife's father, William Retford, was bailiff at Ashley Arnewood. Naish means 'at an ash'. The way to the beach is Chewton Bunny, the latter a word possibly meaning 'reed stream'. The Priory Cartulary refers in 1305 to 'la Bonye', spelt the same on a 1588 Armada threat map. Thomas Coale had 200 men to guard the area. For a decade early in the 19th century children from Milton Poor House worked here making fusee chains to regulate watches. In the 1840s the owner of the mansion nearby was the brother of the writer, Captain Marryat; hence his 'Children of the New Forest'. For 32 years the Elphinstone family had it, then Major Tinker. A hotel since 1962, it has a superb reputation, receiving the Egon Ronay Gold Plate in 1976.

16. The ford over the Walkford stream is shown here in its lovely wooded setting, looking from the west towards Milton up Gore Road on the right. The left hand lane leads to the farm, now Edgar's, managed by Mr. Dolbear. That is out of sight, to the left. The carter's horses are enjoying the cooling water, which looks at least a foot deep where they are. Cyclists, pedestrians and women with prams have a dry passage available over the footbridge. This applied also at the bottom of Golden Hill where the Danes Stream formed the boundary with Hordle. There too the word 'bunny' was used in some church documents. To the right, up Gore Road, there was a brick works in the early years of this century, just in Stem Lane.

Barton Court, Barton-on-Sea.

17. This shows Barton Court from the south-east. The oldest part, still extant, is that to the right. It was the holiday home of the Dent family in the 19th century, till Mr. Dent died in 1891. Within five years the land was planned for housing development. The left section of the Court was a southwards extension made by Mrs. White to her hotel before the First World War; this part was removed about 1922 because of cliff erosion. Today, in parts, there are only 8 feet left in front of the main building. The other photo is of Mrs. Dent, who built a Baptist chapel and an infant school 100 yards from her house. In 1913 her family sold for £118 her collection of Barton fossils to the Bournemouth Natural History Society. One daughter became the Countess of Harrowby, her husband being a grandson of Lord Bute, builder of the first Highcliff Castle. The Baptist ministers were in turn: Mr. Martin, Mr. Crouch and Mr. Scammell. The school mistress was Miss Shave.

18. Volunteers who were camping in the Forest have just been bathing in front of Barton Court Hotel and are wheeling their bikes up the zig-zag path from the beach, which was normally for hotel patrons only. The year is 1902. The large letters of wood 'Barton on Sea Hotel' were carved by Mr. Bushby who lived just east of the village school. Notice the wooden supports to hold back the stones of the beach. Another photograph, taken the same day, shows the soldiers bathing. Twelve years later hundreds more soldiers were to occupy the hotel and huts on its land, as Barton became a convalescent camp. Hosking's Gap, one cutting to the beach, is named after a later estate developer who spent £500 on trying to stabilize the cliff between 1922 and 1937.

19. This photo of the beach at Barton was taken about 1909. In the distance can just be discerned the cliffs of the Isle of Wight to the east of the Needles. The huts here belonged to Barton Court Hotel. At that time other photos show that the beach was very shingly. The photo indicates a gentle slope, bound by grasses, to the base of the cliff. Fossils are found in the blue clays. There have been a few wrecks here. A Russian grain ship was wrecked at Chewton in 1838 and Jacob Uckorar was drowned; he was buried in our churchyard, where now a dozen Eastern European refugees lie. In 1844 the 'Kent', a steamer, was wrecked at Becton, and in 1921 the 'Nutlow' a ketch of 300 tons was beached at Barton, as was the 'Lamorna', a treasure-seeker, in 1951.

Barton Court from W.

20. Barton Court is depicted from the west in this postcard of about 1906 by F. Stuart, whose horse and trap for carrying his equipment have been brought to near the cliff edge. In the distance are the Needles. Almost all the Barton Court buildings in this photograph have now gone, many pulled down because of erosion. Besides the Dents at Barton Court, till 1891, the Bursey family lived at Barton Cliff till 1895. There are murals in the church to this family and the oldest graveyard tomb stone is of a Bursey in 1715. Barton Lane and Becton Lane were drives to and from Barton Court and the farm close to its eastern corner. Dilly Lane led to the other farm further east by some 200 yards. That belonged to the Crossley-Dampier estate. West Barton, for centuries, belonged to Winchester College. Incidentally, Barton Court Hotel had its own vehicle to collect visitors from the station; Mr. E. Manuel was the coachman.

21. These are the six terraced Coastguard Cottages, built in 1868 in Barton Lane, with the officer's house on the west. Smuggling was rife from 1700 to the 1830s. Sometimes hundreds of tubs were landed in a night. Riding officer Bursey was killed in 1780, and a Lulworth youth, Francis Fooks aged 17, was shot in 1832; he lies in our churchyard. Coast guards replaced riding officers, their first station-long since gone-being on the cliff edge. In a 1859 Directory J. Allard, R.N. coast guard, was listed among the gentry. In 1880 there were a petty officer and seven men. J. Brown was the officer till 1900 when J. Lundberg took over till closure in 1908. W. Shave, born in 1863, as a boy knew an old soldier, Mr. Hunt, who lived at the Coastguard cottages when aged 100, an age Mr. Shave reached. He said that there were, apart from these cottages, only nine cottages in Barton in 1870.

22. This photo shows Barton Court Avenue in the 1920s, before the Urban District Council was set up; so the road is of gravel still, without a coating of tar. The Rector, Mr. Kelsall, was involved in planting trees on each side of this road, which had been cut across the fields of Barton Court Estate in the mid-1890s. Mrs. Brown dug up a Roman coin in her garden on the left of the picture, at no. 60 (as it now is). Bronze Age urns have been found on the ridge to the right. The second Barton Golf Course of 1910 used both sides of this road almost to the Highlands Road and Moorland Avenue crossing.

23. The Grand Marine Hotel, united as one building in 1910 as an overflow from Barton Court, was commandeered by the army when war came in 1914 – displacing 250 guests from the hotel complex. Barton Convalescent Camp was set up for British troops, then Indians were sent here largely suffering from dysentery; many of these had first been in Mont Dore Hospital at Bournemouth, the building that is now the Town Hall. There are other photos showing the Indians fraternising with 'Tommies' and with local lads, both at Barton and near the station. One of the latter has nine at the kneeling-firing position, with their rifles pointing at the camera and another fourteen standing behind, surrounding an English boy and young girl in a boater. The hotel changed its name to Barton Chase some ten years or so ago, and is controlled by the Country-wide Holidays' Association. The Marine Bar is next door.

24. At a dangerous period in the war, in June 1917, the obelisk in honour of the Indian troops who had convalesced here was erected, paid for by subscriptions from the staff. Mr. H. Drew's firm erected it, with the aid of some British troops. His photo shows the scaffolding; a card states that it had been made in Plymouth. The Drew firm built hundreds of homes in Milton. Another photo shows the unveiling on 10 July 1917, with hundreds of troops on parade. Later post cards show the Dome Restaurant and the obelisk. There is only one other memorial to the Indians in England, though many Indians were also at Milford and Bournemouth, and a ghat for cremation was made near the hutted hospital at Brockenhurst. The parish War Memorial Cross was dedicated in September 1920 and deeds for the Memorial Recreation Ground were drawn up by November. Field Marshal Sir John Dill's name is listed as among our Second World War dead.

M.C.A. HUT. VIEW ON VERANDAH   BARTON-ON-SEA

25. There are several pictures of the hutted Convalescent Camp at Barton, some showing a scattering of off-duty troops, others with hundreds on parade. This photograph has been chosen because it has the two senior Army doctors seated under the verandah of the YMCA hut, depicted in another photo as having three long skylights. The officers are Lt. Col. Chaytor-White and Lt. Col. Mawson, both of the Indian Army Medical Corps. Their names are inscribed on the Obelisk, and there is a mural plaque to one in the church. Lt. Col. Russell, whose daughter still lives in Milton, had retired just before the war; he gave his services here. Mr. J.D. Banks has just died in Lymington. He was the son of the radiographer captain: as a baby he had lived in Barton wood road.

26. This is the front page of a monthly magazine for the British troops at Barton after the Indians had left. Other issues had photos of the two senior officers on the covers. Sergeant Johnson of the office staff was the editor. Many sketches were excellent, such as one 'Tommie' standing on the cliff edge as it collapses with him on it. 'My stay at Barton is coming to an end.' The camp had some 'firsts' for the area. This is our first paper by eleven years; 'Flicks' were shown here and sports' meetings were held at which troops and civilians could compete. Local people, like Major and Mrs. Chawner, helped to put on concerts, called 'Whizz Bang' concerts, and pierrot shows.

27. This is a photo of Milton Volunteers during the First World War. At the back, from left to right: Pope, Harrison, Jeffery and Rolfe. Second row: Barnes, Baggs, Griffiths, Hatfield, Beal, Weir, Buchan, Frampton, Powell and Price. Third row: May, Kirkman (chemist), Alcock, Miller, Dr. Hunter Woods (the officer), Barker, Skoyles (auctioneer), Spackman (station master) and Statter, Front row: Ford, Rose, Chipperfield (grocer), Read (coal merchant), Payne, Matthews, Wells and Edgar Corbin. There are similar photos of the Home Guard of the Second World War, such as Lieut. Stedman, Sgt. F. Pitt and 43 of No. 2 platoon.

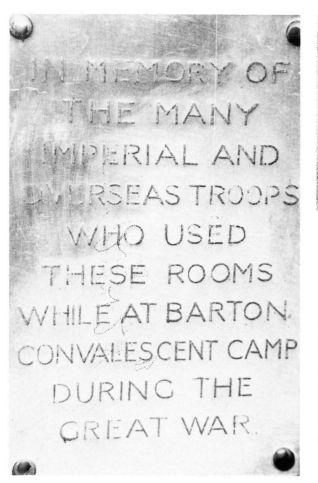

IN MEMORY OF THE MANY IMPERIAL AND OVERSEAS TROOPS WHO USED THESE ROOMS WHILE AT BARTON CONVALESCENT CAMP DURING THE GREAT WAR.

MARCONI'S WIRELESS TELEPHONE STATION FOR COMMUNICATION WITH AIRCRAFT.

THIS STONE WAS LAID BY MISS W. J. VAN HOYTEMA ON 15TH DECR 1919.

GEO. SHEARS & SONS LTD CONTRACTORS, BOURNEMOUTH.

28. These photos should speak for themselves. The brass plaque was attached till 1984 to the door post of the shop at the west end of the Pantiles group of shops that had been built about 1908. This shop (Mann's) is now demolished. The stone inscription is set into the north side of no. 70 bungalow in Sea Road, near the Methodist Church that was to be opened in March 1932. A small airfield had been planned for west Barton. Marconi himself, of course, had lived in south-west Hampshire near Fawley for a short time at the beginning of the century, when he used Lymington steamers to send and receive wireless messages across the waves to a base at Alum Bay. Mr. Marlow, father of the bootmender, had worked for Marconi there.

29. The barns and pond of Little Gore farm make a peaceful setting. There is a story that about 150 years ago the owner sank some tubs of brandy in this pond to avoid the Revenue men. The name 'Moonrakers' for Wiltshire men comes from the story of a farmer, caught raking for submerged tubs, put on his best country-bumpkin act and said he was raking for the moon, reflected in the water. The farm house, with dentils, so probably of about 1780, still stands, but the fields have been used for housing development in the last twenty years. Opposite now are Arnewood School and Sports' complex. Further along Gore Road (meaning 'triangle of land') used to stand Bramble's farm and a cottage inscribed 'I.B.B.1864'. Sammy Miller's Motor Cycle works and Museum are there now. Winchester College has over 40 mediaeval deeds relating to Gore. Stem Lane is mentioned twice by 1360; it leads now to our industrial estate.

30. This photograph, from his granddaughter Lady Lucas, shows the Hon. Auberon Herbert two years before he died in 1906. Called by his biographer 'crusader for liberty', he was a son of the 3rd Earl of Carnarvon; he was years in advance of his time in his interests — archaeology, improved farming, cycling, camping and an anxiety to improve the lot of farm workers, giving them 2/- a week above the normal wage. He lived at Ashley Arnewood from 1873 till a year after his wife died in 1886. He brought Joseph Arch from Suffolk to encourage local labourers to form a Union. For a week every year till the year of his death he offered free meals to people in the area, including gipsies. He is buried in the Forest nearby. He refused to have a fire in his room and insisted on a window being open. When the 'Shakers' (see no. 31) were ejected from their settlement, he gave shelter in his barn to 30 women and children.

31. This is Mrs. Mary Girling, leader of the 'Children of God'; she claimed to be Christ in female form and had moved from London to Forest Lodge in Vaggs Lane, Hordle, half a mile over the parish boundary in January 1872 with 12 disciples. Such was the power of her hypnotic call and the promise it gave of eternal life that within a year about 120 local people, many from Ashley, joined her, bringing their household goods and cattle. Husband and wife now lived as brother and sister. In their ecstasy they often danced, so gained the nick-name of 'Shakers'. On Sundays the women wore white dresses, but for working they wore trousers, regarded as shocking at the time. When they were ejected on 15th December 1874 in a blizzard, some local farmers and gentry, such as Mr. Dent and the Hon. Auberon Herbert, gave shelter. Their camp moved to Little Vaggs, then to Tiptoe, where she died ('Jesus first and last') on 18th September 1886. The remnants of her flock waited for her to rise from the dead.

Lower Ashley, New Milton. 8485

32. Lower Ashley is shown here about 1908. The ford is over a tributary of the Danes Stream. This means 'valley' stream, but Victorians linked it with the Danes, so the Ordnance Survey put a battle sign on maps. The Danes Stream is the boundary between Milton and Hordle, a name that means 'hoard hill', probably because Roman coins were found here in early Saxon times. The lane leads to Downton, spelt 'Duneketon' in the middle ages, probably meaning 'sparrows' farm'. When the main part of Milton church was being pulled down in the 1830s, Hordle Church was being demolished near the cliff and rebuilt near the village centre inland. 12 'Shakers' were buried at the north-east corner of the present Hordle Church. In west-Ashley mediaeval pottery sherds were found by Scouts digging drains near their hut beside the road to Drew's gravel pits.

33. This was the first Baptist Chapel in Ashley. There is evidence of a Baptist ministry, linked with Lymington, as early as 1809 at Ashley. By 1820 a mud-walled chapel had been built; extensions were made in 1845, to be demolished in 1961. Photos of the chapel interior show a high pulpit with plaques on the wall at each side commemorating the services of Thomas Taylor (bailiff at Ashley Clinton), deacon for 50 years till his death in 1886, and of George Peckham, deacon for 60 years, dying in 1861 aged 77. The tablets are now in the new chapel. The strength of the Baptist cause here and the insistence of the Hon. Auberon Herbert ensured that the day school, built in 1879, was non-sectarian. George Peckham's father started the Baptist cause with services in his cottage; he himself allowed a barn to be used. H. Perkins (baker) married his daughter, and their daughters married F. Holes and the Rev. E. Edginton.

34. The second, present, Baptist Chapel at Ashley was built near the cross roads in 1899. A school room was added in 1905, largely through the generosity of the baker, H. Perkins. His house, on the top of Golden Hill, is now Ashley Lodge Nursing Home, with many extensions since 1982. The corner house replaced a thatched cottage and workshop of Mr. Carter, who moved to Manor Road. The energetic and much liked pastor from 1892 to 1909 was the Rev. E. Edginton, whose influence was felt throughout the village. He is shown on a photo of the leaders of the chapel in about 1909. Those with him were J. Lane, H. Perkins, F. Holes (baker), A. Skoyles (auctioneer), E. Peckham and George Avery (head of Ashley School, 1892-1924). A Junior School was built after the Second World War between the chapel and the old school. It is now for infants, as the juniors have moved into what was the Secondary School from 1939 to the 1970s.

35. Vine Cottage makes a lovely picture. It stands in Belmont Road, Ashley; family tradition is that it was only about a dozen years old when this picture was taken. It is of cob. Some members of the Browning family who lived here were attracted to Mrs. Girling's sect and she herself is reputed to have preached here. Her closest follower was Mr. Osborne, who helped to write the account of her in the Dictionary of National Biography. His daughter married Mr. Read, the Ashley coal merchant, and their daughter married Mr. Cecil Foot, the auctioneer and great worker for the Baptist movement, as well as for the bowling club. It may be that Mr. Osborne owned some land at the east end of 'Tower Road' that led to its change of name to Osborne Road. It is most regrettable that the block of flats built in the last ten years at the west end of the road spells the name with a 'u'.

Upper Ashley, New Milton. 8482.

36. This is Ashley Common Road (the common having been enclosed in 1862). On the right is the Anglican Chapel of 1904, called St. Peter's from 1915. The 1888 railway goes under the road in a cutting. A corrugated Hall was built nearer the road. Then in 1957 the present fine church, designed by Sir Ninian Comper's son, was built on the same site. Church Magazines recall that before 1900 there was a tiny Mission hall at Ashley, then another was built as a lean-to against the house of the curate, the Rev. F. Atwood, at the north end of this road where there is a multiple road junction. This was pulled down in 1963 to make way for 'The Woodpecker'. This year the gravel pits on the east of the road are being built up for housing. (In 1884 Bashley Common Road was called Shaves Lane and St. John's Road was then Marlpit Lane.)

37. Ashley Clinton mansion was the home from about 1800 of the Waterloo general, Sir Henry Clinton. He was the son of our Commander in Chief in the War of American Independence. A mural tablet in our church records his life; he died in 1829. Although the house is in Milton, much of the estate is in Hordle and the family were lords of the manor there, with deeds back to the mid-17th century. Soon after the last of his line died, in 1956, 22 of the family's army uniforms became the foundation of the Army Museum display at Camberley. Documents relating to Sir Henry's father's campaigns were sold to America. Note the Water Tower and Observatory. Fire destroyed the mansion. North of this estate, also in both parishes, was the Stanleys Estate, named after the owner in 1670. In late Victorian times Mrs. Gunning-Sutton lived there; then her granddaughter, Lady Lilian Liddell sold it to Lady Harpur Crewe in 1901. It is now a Country Park and Hotel.

BASHLEY AND ASHLEY ROAD.

38. The photograph was taken about 1928 from Marks Lane looking towards Cull Lane across what local people call 'Pig stye corner'. A vestige of the grass at the centre remains, but the cottage on the right has gone. The sign points left to Sway, Lyndhurst and Lymington, and right to Christchurch. Amazingly, the road number is given as B 3056. Today it is B 3055, as a sign on the main Fernhill Lane junction states. Maps and documents of the late Victorian period show that some lanes in the Bashley area changed their names with the owners of farmsteads. South of Fernhill crossroads belonged to Winchester College for hundreds of years, while land in Bashley – to the north – had belonged to Christchurch Priory from soon after the Conquest. Presumably gates were across the roads here for centuries.

39. Laurence Housman, brother of poet 'A.E.', was himself a prolific author, especially of plays. He and his artist-engraver sister Clemence came to 'Greycot', 11 King's Road, Ashley in 1913. Here he wrote playlets about St. Francis for children, and here he met two of Mrs. Girling's first twelve disciples, one being 'Lizzie' Chase. Their story led him to write his novel 'The Sheepfold' (1918) and to give a brief talk on the radio in 1949 (reproduced in 'The Listener') repeating their story that the remnants of the 'Shakers' waited by their 'Mother's' grave at Hordle for her to rise from the dead, and that one child's suggestion that they should move the flowers was acted on. It is a pity a few of his dates were wrong. This gentle cultured pair left Ashley for Street in Somerset, where he died in 1959, the 'last of the Victorians'. 'Greycot' was taken over by Mr. Spackman, even better known than the Housmans, as he had been station master for over 25 years.

40. Miss Dora Harlow is on her Ashley milk round about 1922. She worked for her relative, John Brewer of 'Ivy Holm' of Hare Lane Dairies. Now a widow, Mrs. Gordon lives in Hordle; she was born on 31 December 1900. She used to deliver milk to the Housmans (no. 39), and kept up a casual correspondence with them till his death. Major Symons, nephew of Housman, is 90; he is President of the Housman Society and lives in Lymington. John Brewer's step-father, Eli Corbin, worked on Sway Tower built 1879-1885 by A. Peterson with no scaffolding nor re-inforcement. The top was completed by Tom Ackland, whose daughter (Mrs. Rose Corbin) died at 98 in 1976; they had worshipped at the Victoria Mission Hall, Bashley. Her husband, Herbert, was a gardener for Lady Cooper at Ossemsley Manor in north Milton, now nine luxury flats. Incidentally, Mr. John Farwell began his farming 'Empire' with a milk round from one cart in 1889.

41. Veal's Corner in Bashley is named after the family whose house – now gone – is shown on the east side of the main road as it bends sharply towards 'The Rising Sun' (rebuilt 1903). This photo, taken from New Lane, looks across to Veal's house. The white double cottage on the right has been halved since the Second World War to afford room for a new house. The right hand section has been empty since the death in 1984 of Mrs. V. Feltham. The left turning goes to Ossemsley (mentioned in no. 40). In 1670 Thomas Stevens put in for Forest rights on his 172 acres. General Roberts was there in the 1840s, then Major Murray, who died in 1907. (There is a mural in our church.) Sir Alfred Cooper came next; his widow stayed for a few years. It became a Country Club in the 1970s, and in the 1980s has been altered to give nine luxury flats. It is a fine battlemented building. 'Osanlea' of 984, 'Oselei' in 1086, has been identified as Ossemsley, but I think it was an unidentified manor in the Boldre area.

Post Office, Bashley.

42. This is the Bashley Post Office and general shop on the west side of the main road and just below Veal's corner that no longer makes a severe right turn. Nearly opposite is the garage of the Loader family, who were for years the blacksmiths. Mr. E. James was the sub post master in the early years of this century, when it was built. In 1907 St. John's Anglican chapel was built down the lane beside the garage site. Bashley ('Baylokesleya', meaning 'Bagloc's woodland clearing') was granted by Edward the Confessor to a thegn in 1053, according to one of only three Saxon charters in the unpublished Priory Cartulary. By 1066 it was held by a secular canon of Christchurch called Alsi in Domesday; till the Dissolution it was held by the Priory and was separated from Winchester College Fernhill lands by a gate across the road till the early years of this century. It was not in 'Rodedic' Hundred like most neighbouring manors, but was in 'Egheiete' like 'Tuinam' (Christchurch).

Wootton
Post
Office

43. The sub Post Office at Wootton was opened in 1855, presumably to serve the gentry in the north parts of Milton. Mr. Wallace ran it, then his daughter, Mrs. Ivemy, from the 1890s. Miss Russell was here in the 1920s, before Mr. Wooldridge, father of Ian, the sports' writer. About 1900 Mr. Bran brought on the mail from Everton in his trap. Directories give times of collections. Wootton had a Primitive Methodist Chapel and a National School, the heads from 1880s being Bassett, Smith and Coghlan; he was head when the school burnt down in 1914. Wootton was 'Odetune' ('farm in the wood') in 1086. The Forest bounds were always here, marked with a bank, which became 'Rodedic' Hundred moot in north Hinton. Col. Harman lived at Wootton Hill, nearby was the painting hut of Professor A. Seaby, whose grandson in the 1950s found Mesolithic flints of about 10,000 B.C. in a gravel pit here.

Fernhill Lane

44. This is Fernhill Lane from the north, looking towards the farm house that became a school in 1919. The lane is still a lovely entry to the town and station. There has been an important house here from late Saxon times. By 1086 it was one of Earl Roger's manors; then the Farnhull family took their name from it. In 1420 it was the head manor of John Fromond's Estate that he willed to Winchester College, to provide rents to pay for the clothes of 16 choir boys. His box of deeds take leases back to 1199; there are over 300 mediaeval manuscripts relating to Fernhill, Gore, West Barton and lands in Christchurch, etc. The College began to sell lands only two years after the railway came. Mr. Kennard farmed here (hence Kennard Road), then 'Daddie' Tee, etc. Miss Clarke and Miss Macnamara moved their Branksome Girls' School here in 1919 and changed its name to Fernhill Manor. In 1985 it appointed its first headmaster.

Fernhill Lane, Milton

45. This is one of many postcards taken about 1907 of Fernhill Lane; the embowering trees, little ford and pedestrian bridge make a very pleasant picture, especially when people and horsed vehicles can give life. Colonel Ubsdell of Great Ballard, slightly to the north, gave the lake to the village. His mother, daughter of a famous American engineer, as a tiny child was nursed by President Abraham Lincoln, in the 1860s. The lake is now beautifully cared for. Recently a document has come to light that proves that Col. Thomas White, whose family lived at Fiddleford in north Dorset, lived here. His memorial and sword are in the church, and his widow gave the lovely communion silver in 1726/7. The College offered for sale 131 plots along Kennard Road in April 1890, and 57 plots were offered in 1926 to line Marley Avenue. Manor Road (meaning Fernhill Manor) was the first new road.

46. This fine photo shows a group of Indian soldiers on New Milton Station in 1915. Note the barley-sugar twist of the gas lamp and the amount of vegetation behind the men. On the back of the photo is a stamp: 'Passed by Press Bureau', then 'Copyright. Topical Press Agency, London; Copyright in U.S.A. and Canada.' The words typed were presumably used in a newspaper at the time. They read: 'At New Milton a contingent of our brave Indian soldiers left to rejoin their comrades in the firing line. After recovering from their wounds they are glad to go out again to fight for their King Emperor.' It is very much to be doubted if such words could have been used after the carnage of 1916 in the trenches.

47. A William Adams' London and South Western locomotive 02 (0-4-4) engine no. 222 stands on the line about 1906. This Railway Company had built 'Castleman's corkscrew' line through the forest to Ringwood in 1847 with a station called — at first — Osmondley Ford, later Christchurch Road, but known mostly as Holmsley. Although only half a mile from the parish bounds, it had had little influence. The main line changed everything. The Holmsley line was closed in May 1963. In 1964 a ticket was found stamped: AU 22 .88./ L & S W R/ Christchurch to MILTON/ Third Class Parliamentary. This last word refers to the 1844 Act-1d per mile. In 1906 fares from Waterloo to Bournemouth Central were: 1st class 31/6; 2nd class 19/9; 3rd class 16/-; breakfast 2/6. Note the 1900 Water Tower in the background.

48. The Railway's steam bus is leaving the station and sending up a cloud of dust from the macadam road about 1906, just before it was withdrawn on 15 September because it got stuck so often in ruts on its route between Lymington and New Milton via Milford-on-Sea. Hamilton Ellis's 'The Southern Railway' (1956) states that one of two steam buses used was a Clarkson of 32 h.p. They had come into service only 14 months before, on 19th July 1905. There exist fine close-up shots of the two different buses on the slope of Lymington High Street, but this seems to be the only one taken in New Milton. The line of shops on the left, including Elliott's of Lymington, was built in 1904/5. It was a Royal Blue horse bus that used to meet passengers for Bournemouth at Holmsley till 1862, when the route from Ringwood south to Christchurch was opened.

49. The photographer is looking down Station Road as the whole village turn out in their Sunday best for the Hospital Sunday Parade from the village green, to collect money to help the local hospitals. The date, judging from the ladies' picture hats, the men's boaters and the boy's Eton collar, is probably about 1913. If so, a year later many men would have been in khaki. Lymington and other local bands usually played and Friendly Society banners were paraded too. 'The Christchurch Times' used to list amounts collected in the churches, etc. People paid a few pence a week to cover eventualities that might involve hospital treatment. Kirkman's chemist shop has a huge pear-shaped lamp; he came in 1907 to the opposite side. He was to become Mayor of Lymington and retired in 1960 owning eight shops; his death came in 1967 when he was 91. White and Pitman, drapers and milliners, occupy the premises opposite the Post Office.

THE LANDLORD OF THE
WILTON HOTEL.

50. This photo of about 1903 concentrates on Hugh Wyeth's Milton Hall by Station bridge. It was used for dances, meetings, concerts, etc. For a few years Mr. Wyeth and the rector ran a youth club here. The Wilts and Dorset Bank, open three times a week, occupied the right hand section. Misselbrook and Westons had a double shop just visible on the left. Opposite was Harrison's tobacconist shop, later to be Kirkman's chemist shop, and Percy Beal's shop is near the Post Office, run since 1901 by the Novelles. Mr. Skoyles, the estate agent and auctioneer, took over the Hall. His home was Gore Grange, later occupied by Mr. Jowitt, whose wife – being a Wedgwood – had some nice pottery. Mr. Cecil Foot took over the Auction Room; now it is used by Porter and Clark, the seed merchants, who have moved from opposite. The sketch is of Hugh Wyeth, enjoying the auction of plots at Milton Hotel in 1890. He died in 1900, the first to foresee that Milton would become a town.

New Milton, Hants

51. This photo was taken from the top of the Water Tower, built in 1900 by the West Hants Water Company. The railway bridge and Milton Hotel are shown right centre, with Fred Keeping's Motor and Cycle Works nearer us, beside the double shop where Mrs. Newhook had her sub Post Office and confectionery, before Novelles took over in 1901, till they moved later that year to the Whitefield corner shop, just off the picture. Wyeth's Hall, then partly used as a bank, is shown, as is his hotel behind which there is just a sprinkling of the housing development that was to quicken in the 1920s and again in the 1970s. Captain Roach later built a garage opposite Fernhill Manor school; this became Cooper's, till it closed for housing development in 1985.

S.F.S. SERIES   BARTON COURT ROAD AND ELM AVENUE, NEW MILTON, FROM THE AIR   No. 1428

52. This aerial photo of the early 1920s shows Station Road going up the picture, with Barton Court Road from the left corner meeting the main road at Captain Broach's Homefield School and a space opposite where the 'Waverley' cinema was built in 1929. Elm Avenue slips off diagonally to the left, with Whitefield Road plainly seen in the left corner. In the last 18 months many houses on the north side of Elm Avenue have been demolished to make way for a large extension of the car park behind the corner shop, namely Alderson's. Mr. R. Alderson was Lymington Mayor when the Queen came in 1966 past this corner on her way to Lymington. In 1974 he was the first Chairman of the New Forest District Council. There were no shops south of the main cross roads. Hayward's farm is shown – now the site of builders' merchant, Roberts Adlard.

53. This shows Novelle's sub Post Office on the corner of Whitefield Road. They had moved here in 1901, when it was built, from their shop just over station bridge, which Mrs. Emma Newhook had managed as sub post mistress since 1895, though she may have started that job in a cottage just south of the cross roads to Old Milton Road. It was Mrs. Newhook who put up the name *New* Milton sub Post Office, a name adopted in May 1897 by the Railway. The Post Office building stood on its own for a year or two, maps show. Note its ornate superstructure and French chateau spire. Bank corner, to be built opposite for the Wilts and Dorset (later Lloyd's), copied the style, the two facing buildings making a pleasant Edwardian picture.

54. Christmas 1906 has brought so many huge parcels that Mr. and Mrs. Novelle have had to sort it out on the pavement. They are pictured here, as well as Mr. Patience, the postman, about to set off on his round. Although the roads were not tarred till the mid-1920s, it is interesting to note that there is a curbed pavement. Mr. Novelle continued as post master till 1922. The present main Post Office was built in 1933. Now a queue forms there every Thursday morning, pension day. Reading an article of mine in 'The New Milton Advertiser' about early postal frankings showing 'New Milton' a kind reader, Mr. Tanner of Kenya, sent a photo-copy of a stamp franked: NEW MILTON/ PM/ NO 2/ 00/. That is, 2 November 1900, when Mrs. Emma Newhook was sub post mistress. So far I have been unable to contact relatives or descendants of Mrs. Newhook.

55. This is Milton School's football team of 1923, with the head, Mr. Barker. They are, left to right (back): T. West, W. Keeping, W. Bowring, F. Legg and J. West. Middle: J. Martin, G. Glassbrook and R. Welch. Front: N. Clark, J. Powell, L. Matthews (killed in 1940 air-raid), S. Partridge and G. Dunford. They are outside the hutted school, in use from 1919, when Mr. Barker brought the school from the middle of the road by the 'George'. The old school was pulled down at Easter 1931. This hut is one of the ex-army huts erected as classrooms on Winchester College land in Gore Road. By 1833 Milton had five daily schools in cottages. Mr. J. Bursey gave land so a National School was built for £174, money coming from Sir G. Rose and Sir G. Tapps, etc. The first head was J. Olding, with his sister; both were paid £15 a year, with use of the school house. Heads from 1880 were Hayward, Hamp, Quinion, then Barker. The huts were removed for housing in 1983.

56. Ashley School was founded in 1879 at Hare Lane corner, and was closed in July 1985, its last years as a special school. Largely through A. Herbert it was non-denominational in this Baptist strong-hold. The outside plaque is indecipherable, but one inside refers to E. Jenkins, M.P. This 1920 photo shows the head, Mr. Avery (1892-1924) with, back, left to right: E. Harris, F. Pond, J. Sargeant, S. Rickman, M. Mellish and S. Moore. Second row: S. Black, I. Payne, R. Bourne, M. Sherred and F. Boyce. Third row: L. Penny, ?, G. Corbin, E. Whitcher, ? and D. Saltaire. Front: S. Miller, G. Bowring, E. Feltham, T. Blake, E. Browning and S. Hoad. The little photo is of William Retford, at school from 1879. He became England's finest violin bow maker, with a book on the craft in 1964. A new Junior/Infant School was built in 1951, the year Mr. Avery died, at 88. Milton's first Secondary School was opened at Ashley in 1939, Mr. Wakefield being head. It merged with Gore in 1970; its building is now the Junior School.

57. Wootton was a National School, being aided by the Church of England National Society; it was also used as a chapel. Note that the left end was thatched. A tiny belfry was erected there and a porch from the left window, as later photos show. On a June Sunday in 1914 most was gutted by a fire after lightning struck. Mr. H. Coghlan was the head, following Mr. H. Smith. Inspectors' reports in late Victorian times had been largely critical, but big improvements came from Mr. Smith's time. A later head was Mr. Carr, whose son became master of St. Anthony's College at Oxford. After the fire the school moved to the 'Iron' Church opposite Vaggs lane, then to ex-army huts on the old site. The new school was built over the parish boundary double bank in Tiptoe. (Tiptoe is named from a Normandy village from which had come a mediaeval family. Other members lived in Barton.)

58. The earliest private school that has survived, though under a different name and on a different site, is Branksome college for girls, founded about 1893 by the Miss Hawkins at 'Copseland', then soon at 'Branksome', both close to Ashley Arnewood. Fees were: resident, over 12 years of age, 50 guineas; day pupils, over 12 years of age, 15 guineas. Tennis and croquet were played. French, piano, needlework and Swedish drill were in the prospectus, that also mentioned cycling or walking in the afternoon. In 1913 the school was bought by Miss Clarke and Miss Macnamara; six years later they took over Fernhill Manor house and changed the name of the school. Branksome Close now marks the site of the school's second position. In 1985 the school broke new ground by appointing a headmaster.

59. This is a school now forgotten, though the building is well-known, for since 1954 it has been a home for displaced people from Eastern Europe. Mr. Baldock M.A. built it as Hengistbury School for boys on a site, he claimed, 'recommended by doctors'. Pupils were drilled daily. Mrs. Baldock had a trained matron to help her. In 1913 the sisters, Miss M. & Miss C. Butterworth, turned it into Barton Court School for girls; their father taught tennis. When the First World War came it was taken over by the Convalescent Camp. The girls' school then continued till about 1924, when it became a boys' school for a few years before becoming a hotel in the 1930s, till requisitioned in the Second World War. Then it was a Nurses' Rest Home. Today it contains an Eastern Orthodox Chapel and was been visited in 1966 by Prince S. Aga Khan, then commissioner for refugees. Many refugees now lie in our churchyard, their graves marked by a diagonal over the cross. In the 1920s there lived next door the Redmayne family; a daughter was at the school and one son became Tory party chairman, Lord Redmayne.

FURZIE CLOSE.

60. Furzie Close Preparatory School off Becton Lane was founded in 1909 by Mr. Stubbs. A bad fire hit the school. After the Second World War Mr. Cox's Dorset school, Durlston Court, founded in 1926, came after being in Cumberland during the war. It too suffered a fire. Another local boys' preparatory school was Great Ballard, founded in 1895 off Fernhill Lane, under Mr. Colborn. The Duke of Connaught visited it when Mr. Kefford was head, in 1935. The school moved to Camberley during the Second World War. Edinburgh House School took over the site, after evacuation to Somerset and Oxford. 'Speedwell' was a small school for boys on the north side of Manor Road, run by the Kershaw family. One pupil, John Heath Stubbs, won the Queen's gold medal for poetry in 1970; one poem is about Milton churchyard. Mr. C.T. Curry, editor/owner of 'The New Milton Advertiser', 1932-1966 sent his two sons to 'Speedwell'; they now run this fine paper, begun by Kirby Wynne in 1928.

61. From Neolithic times the main industry along the south coast was farming. Being such a common sight, there are few photos of men ploughing. This photo shows Mr. Henry Cheyney at work on Naish Farm, owned by the Joy family. He lived at Chewton (see no. 15). One old resident recalls when the whole of the coastal area of Barton, now filled with houses, was once a sea of corn. 90 year old Mr. Breaker of Hordle remembers steam ploughing with two stationary engines, some 250 yards apart in west Ashley when he was a boy, and the Spencer family – from whom Spencer Road is probably named – has a small nursery opposite Ashley Arnewood. In parts of Barton the mediaeval strips seem to have been 11 yards wide, but Ashley Secondary School field had strips of half that width (rod, pole, perch), revealed when snow melted. Mr. John Farwell and his wife Elizabeth (née Burry) rented Church Farm in 1889; eventually they bought up many farms, and their daughters married farmers, Fawcett and Edgar.

62. This is Mr. Charles Loader's smithy in Smithy Lane, Bashley about 1910. He is shown on the right, with his apprentice, Mr. Haskell. Mr. Loader's family now run a garage business on the main road through Bashley, opposite the Post Office. The Brownen family were the smiths in the old village of Milton for many generations, run full time till 1949, and closed in 1954. They used to 'fire the anvil' for big weddings, and for the 1897 Jubilee fired 21 charges. There are photos of the smithies in Highcliffe, that is – in Newtown, which was in Milton parish till 1843. Loader's old home has recently been beautifully renovated, making it a 'picture postcard'. A hundred years ago Charles James was a blacksmith in Bashley and Henry Tudgey in Ashley. Sam Carter was the wheelwright at Ashley Cross Roads till he moved to Manor Road.

63. As soon as the railway reached Milton, advantage was taken of the clay outcrops to set up brick kilns. This photo shows Sam Browning's kilns in Andrew Lane, Ashley. On the left is Christopher Andrew, whose home probably gave its name to the lane. There are two Buckle brothers, an Adams and the lad, George Brain. There were two kilns off Gore Road, one under Morgan Foot on the site now of the Gas Company, and another just on the right over the rail bridge in Stem Lane, run by Mr. Collins, later by Mr. Mitchell. As a young man, Mr. Foot used to walk to Bournemouth to his building jobs. Mr. S. Chappell of London owned kilns at the south end of Spencer Road managed by T. Lloyd from 1889 for over 14 years. John Powell had another site from 1890 till 1907 at least. F. Frampton had kilns in Walkford, and there were others in Byron Road where cement blocks were made in the late 1920s. None is in W. White's article in Hampshire Field Club volume, December 1973.

64. Ashley Post Office and village store are being built in 1897. On the right is Mr. Isaac Corbin who built it and put in his son-in-law, William Talbot, as first postmaster/shopkeeper. A later occupier, Mr. Burbidge, had a bakehouse behind. Another photo shows plasterers and bricklayers, with the tools of their trades, pausing during their work on an unknown house. Isaac Corbin's brother, Eli, built Misselbrook and Weston's double shop on the station approach, as well as other buildings at the beginning of the century. Another well-known early builder was Mr. Powell; Mr. H. Drew came to New Milton in 1907 and built up a very prosperous firm, in which his wife played a prominent part, till their son took over in 1946. She also ran 'Janel', hairdressers. Mr. L. Whitcher was another builder; born in 1888, he was to become a town councillor for twenty years after playing football and cricket for local teams. His firm built the 'Waverley' cinema.

65. This is Miss A. Bateson's wagonette laden with nursery produce on its way to the market. The driver is her manager, Mr. C. Lane, who was to succeed her as the owner of the nursery, in 1928, the year of her death. Anna Bateson was Britain's first professional lady nursery owner. She gained a Botany degree at Cambridge, where her father was master of St. John's College. Her brother William was to be the first director of the John Innes Horticultural Institution, and a F.R.S. She founded her nursery at Bashley in 1892 when she was 29. She was to play a prominent part in the local community as Parish and District Councillor, etc. One retired teacher born in Wootton, who gained a scholarship to Brockenhurst and then went on to Southampton University College, remembers with gratitude the lessons Miss Bateson freely gave her in French.

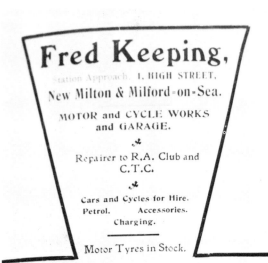

Fred Keeping,
Station Approach, 1, HIGH STREET,
New Milton & Milford-on-Sea.

MOTOR and CYCLE WORKS
and GARAGE.

Repairer to R.A. Club and
C.T.C.

Cars and Cycles for Hire.
Petrol.   Accessories.
Charging.

Motor Tyres in Stock.

66. Fred Keeping's Motor and Cycle Works and Garage occupied a prime position close to the station and Milton Hotel. This photo from a 1910 Guide shows that cycles were his 'bread and butter'; however, he did sell Michelin tyres. He had another garage at Milford. Today this site and the double house next door, used by Mrs. Newhook and then by Mr. Novelle as a sub Post Office, are held by Williams' Motor Garage. The Water Tower, with its castellated battlements in mock-Tudor style and drip moulds over the 'windows', dominates the background from the other side of the railway. Facing it now in Osborne Road is the two storeyed Community Centre. Today seven garages sell petrol in New Milton. Cooper's Fernhill Garage, originally Capt. Roche's, has just been closed for housing development.

67. Mr. C. Dallas's first steam car stands outside his house, Eastley Wootton, just inside the forest. Seated at the back is his man-servant, Jack Card, who went abroad on all his employer's tours. The vehicle is a 'Lifu' of 1899, of 25 h.p. It carried 70 gallons of water and 40 of paraffin, so it could travel for 60 miles, at about 12 m.p.h. He later owned a 9 h.p. Napier of 1902 and an 18 h.p. Napier of 1904, then a 1909 Panhard. Photos exist of all these. Dr. Hunter-Woods, who lived at 'Essendene' on the corner of Tower Road, seems to have been the next owner of a car. Lt. Col. Clinton's first car was a 'Sunbeam' of 1912, Mr. F. Keeping being his chauffeur. From about 1920 there are photos of char-à-banc outings, by the choir, Conservatives to the Isle of Wight (1920), Mr. Drew's firm to Salisbury (1922), etc. At the turn of the century the carrier – with horses – between Lymington and Christchurch was John Saunders, on Monday, Thursday and Saturday.

THE
BARTON TEA HOUSE

BARTON-ON-SEA (Hants).

LUNCHEONS & AFTERNOON TEAS
a Speciality.

HOT AND COLD LUNCHEONS ON SUNDAYS.
Light Refreshments at any time. Moderate Tariff.

Picnic and School Parties Catered for on special terms.

Choice Selection of Home made Cakes.
High class Sweets and Confectionery.

Under the personal supervision of the Proprietresses.

68. This restaurant, opposite the entrance to the Golf Links, was one of the first. By 1910 the new proprietress, Mrs. Z. Furneaux, was also letting apartments and running a Library, linked with Mudie's. The deposit was 2/6; 2d was charged per volume for three days. Its telephone number was 3. The Moslem Gold Dome was added later on the left projection, appropriately facing the Indian memorial. Later came the still existing Barton Cliff Hotel. Once the 1868 Coast Guard Station was closed, in 1908, Mr. Lundberg ran 'Seacroft' on Sea Road as a boarding house. It offered 'stable or motor accommodation' and a bath (hot and cold). The last ten years have seen a proliferation of rest homes, some having been hotels like 'Carlton House', or homes, like Dr. Begg's, later 'Ebenezer House', and Ashley Arnewood. There are now many Nursing Homes, such as 'Windyridge' – once the Coast Guard Officer's House.

69. Milton Urban District Council, set up in 1926, only lasted six years, for in 1932 it was swallowed up by Lymington, to the anger of many people in this area. Despite its short 'reign', it made considerable progress, in lighting, paving, draining and tarring the main roads. This photograph probably dates from about 1928 and shows men taking a brief rest from tarring. Amazingly one man is in white trousers. Left to right are: Frank Corbin, Bill Coles, Charles Buckle, Mr. Broomfield and 'Slippery' Young. It is pleasant to record that there are still a few drain covers with the letters 'M.U.D.C.' for Milton Urban District Council.

70. In the first half of the 19th century Colonel Peter Hawker became this country's most famous wild-fowler through his books and exploits at Keyhaven in nearby Milford. In the last hundred years the best known shooting sportsman (not now a term that would be used by many) in the New Forest, was Mr. Charles Dallas of Eastley Wootton, whose cars have been noted on no. 67. Once again Jack Card is with him in this fine photo. He had left school on the Island when he was ten. His master was to die in his late 90s. In 1927 Mr. Dallas, who also owned a yacht 'Beluga', published his 'New Forest Shooting, past and present'. He lists his 'bag' in the Forest and in Dorset from 1885 to 1926. These are some totals: 1,906 pheasants, 119 hares, 171 partridges, 563 woodcock, 301 snipe, and 8,735 rabbits; in 1760 days of shooting there were a total of 12,084.

71. Within the space of 35 years Barton had three golf courses. The first, of 1897/8 owned by Sir R. Affleck, bart., was from the east end of Barton Court Hotel along the cliff top and was of nine holes, three of which have long since slipped over the edge because of erosion. The professional shown here was probably Mr. E. Kettley; the bearded man was Mr. Handy, a builder and uncle of Arthur Warren, who became the club pro. after a course was constructed inland to the design of Harry Vardon. This second course was opened in 1910 and reached beyond where now is the north-east bend in Barton Drive, as can be seen from a sketch plan in 'The New Milton Advertiser' of 30 April 1960. The present course was opened in 1932; once again it is seeking additional land to replace eroded greens. In October 1985 planners refused to permit addition to its club house because it is such a fine representative of a style now difficult to find.

72. 'Ye Olde Golf Cottage' adjoined the club house of the first course and was run by Miss Place and Miss Lyon-Campbell. In fact it had been the home of the Shave family in the 19th century; there were nine children of whom three lived into their 90s and one, William, died in January 1964 aged 100. I recorded his reminiscences in 'The New Milton Advertiser' then. The Club House for the 1910 course was off Dilly Lane and is now a bungalow, the first six holes being east of Barton Court Avenue, the rest to the west, almost to Sea Road. (Incidentally, the word 'Ye' uses a 19th century misinterpretation of the Saxon symbol called a 'thorn' for 'th', which was written with the left stroke upright, but printers did not have the symbol. 'Ye' and 'Yat' should be read as 'The' and 'That'. Another symbol was for 'th' as in 'thin'; this was written 'D', but with a horizontal line through the upright, as at Breamore Church.)

73. Milton Operatic Society is shown in 'H.M.S. Pinafore'. This Society was founded in 1912 by Major and Mrs. Chawner. They put on 'Patience' and 'Pirates of Penzance', etc. at Milton Hall. Major Chawner who came here in 1906 is in the centre; William Patience (postman, on no. 54) was Dick Deadeye. Also present are the two Miss Haywards, who lived on the east corner at the crossroads; W.E. Kirkman (chemist and later Mayor); Henry Flay; Edward Collier (postman); Mr. Matthews (watch repairer); Tom Browning; Gladys Powell and Mr. Illingworth (labourer). After the First World War, Mr. Avery, head at Ashley school, was bandmaster for Ashley Temperance Band; they wore pill-box hats. In 1917 British troops put on 'Whizz Bang' concerts at Barton and Major Chawner helped with pierrot shows. Miss Baker of Elm Avenue ran the Choral Society; after the First World War the New Forest Players were founded, largely through Mrs. L. Platt. Today there are some 90 clubs of all sorts. The Cricket Club is 100 years old.

74. This is the 'Scala' Cinema in Station Road. Mr. Wilkinson brought this ex-army hut from Christchurch, where the New Zealanders had used it. Built in 1919 for silent films, with the light behind the screen, it was also used for other entertainments, and in 1928 for church services when the parish church was being renovated. Films had been shown two years earlier to the Barton troops who also had their own monthly paper, 'Barton Breezes' (see no. 26). 'The New Milton Advertiser' was not founded till 1928, on 7 June; it cost ½d. That week the 'Scala' was showing a Bebe Daniels and Ben Lyon film. It was demolished in May 1934. Just below where it had stood a stick of bombs on 23 August 1940 devastated many shops, Loveless's being gutted. 24 people died that day, 19 being civilians. The 'Waverley' Cinema opened for 'talkies' in 1929, closing on 1972 with 'Those magnificent men in their flying machines'.

Catholic Church, Int, New Milton. 46.

75. This is 'Our Lady of Lourdes', the Roman Catholic Church in Mount Avenue, built in 1927 (64 ft x 24 ft) when there were less than fifty Catholics here. An anonymous donor paid the £750 needed for the site. When the Bishop of Portsmouth blessed the church, a Weld was present as well as the Catholic Mayor of Lymington, General Newenham. It was the Weld family of Lulworth who paid for the Roman Catholic Church and school in Lymington in 1859. On 20 June 1945 the Second World War's only double V.C., Captain C. Upham, was married here to Mary McTamney by Father F. Pinkney. Mount Avenue is named after the house at the road junction built for the Hallowes brothers. One, a solicitor, used to commute by rail to Southampton. Late in 1907 swearing in gutteral German was heard from the road. It was the Kaiser, whose car had broken down, on his way from Highcliff Castle. The Mount is now divided into flats.

76. Milton Baptist Church, 1910, on Hobart Road (now used as the Hall). The Barton-on-Sea Methodist Church was opened on 23 March 1932, at the junction of Sea and Cliffe Roads, at a total cost of £1,721, including the site cost. The first Minister was the Rev. Charles Speck, who died the following year. The hall was opened in October 1951 and there have been great changes, with rebuilding, since, as Methodism has a strong following here. Almost opposite now is 'The Red Linnet', named after Col. Mew's boat. In the 1930s too there were built Gore Road Evangelical Church and the Evangelical Free Church in Whitefield Road, which has now opposite it the Friends' Meeting House and the First Church of Christ Scientist; both of the latter back on the railway. On Sundays all the various churches and chapels in New Milton are well attended. This is, of course, largely a retirement area.